LES REBELLES Collection
Managing Editors : Danielle Pampuzac and Jean Cormier

Photographs :
René Burri
Chinolope
Raúl Corrales
Saúl Corrales
José A. Figueroa
Alberto Korda
Liborio Noval
Roger Pic
Perfecto Romero
Osvaldo and Roberto Salas
Philippe Séclier
Carlos Torres Cairo
Lucia Zalbidea Muñoz

Thanks to :
Consejo Nacional de las Artes Plásticas de Cuba.
Cubana de Aviación
Fototeca de Cuba.
Oficina Asuntos Históricos del Consejo
de Estado de la Republica de Cuba.
Unión de Escritores y Artistas de Cuba. (UNEAC).

Layout artist :
Ismael Morejón Álvarez

Layout:
Raúl Abelardo Puchades Lopez

Editors:
Saúl Corrales
Carlos Torres Cairo

Printer:
SELVi Artes Gráficas.

Translated from the French :
Patricia Meyer (for Pizano)
Assisted by Edward Cahill

I.S.B.N. 84-607-9547-0
Depósito legal V-5104-2003

CHE
GUEVARA

BY THE PHOTOGRAPHERS
OF THE CUBAN REVOLUTION

RENÉ BURRI, RAÚL CORRALES, CHINOLOPE, ALBERTO FIGUEROA, ALBERTO KORDA
LIBORIO NOVAL, ROGER PIC, PERFECTO ROMERO, OSVALDO AND ROBERTO SALAS

EDICIONES AURELIA
www.cubaimagen.com

El Ché y la sensibilidad

De todas las virtudes que conforman la personalidad de Ernesto Guevara de la Serna, considero que una de las mas importantes, es la gran sensibilidad que lo acompaña en todos los aspectos de su vida.

Esta exquisita sensibilidad se pone de manifiesto en los más dissimiles aspectos de su vida. Aparece en su amor de hijo presente en las cartas a sus padres a quienes tuvo siempre presente a lo largo de su accidentada vida. Se pone de manifiesto ademas su sensibilidad como padre en sus cartas a sus hijos y amigos

Como médico, puso en evidencia su amor al prójimo y que lo manifestó en discursos jiscritos, y que le hacían sentir la necesidad de cambiar el orden establecido, por otro más justo y humano

En su actividad guerrillera, tanto en Cuba, como en El Congo y por último en Bolivia, esta sensibilidad omnipresente, lo llevó a efectuar actos heroicos, salvando vidas tanto de compañeros como de enemigos

1

Che and sensitivity

Of all the virtues of the personality of Ernesto Guevara de la Serna, I believe that one of the most important is his huge sensitivity that accompanied him in every moment of his life.

This extraordinary sensitivity presented itself in different ways. His devotion to his parents was seen in his letters to them; no matter where he was he never forgot them for one instant during his turbulent life. In his letters to his children and his friends his fatherly sensitivity came out. As a doctor he showed the love he had for his fellow man, present in his speeches as well as in his writings. This love pushed him to change the order established by others, to become more just and more humane.

In his activities as a guerrilla, in Cuba, in the Congo and finally in Bolivia, this omnipresent sensitivity led him to realise heroic deeds where he saved the lives of his friends as well as his enemies.

But in this extraordinary man existed another type of sensitivity that became apparent only through being in contact with him, direct and non-stop : the capacity to separate, in his entourage, he who was beautiful from he who was ugly, he who was exceptional from he who was common. This facet of the personality of the "future" Che is illustrated in his taste for photography because it aided him to reveal the differences. This esthetique pleasure has accompanied him even until today where he has become the paradigm of the man who will do everything in his power for the fall of capitalism. A capitalism which at present looks to globalise injustice, poverty and the loss of ethnic values.

To conclude, one can say that this sensitivity permitted him to identify over and over again, and through the means of photography, with the culture of a country like France, a country that he always wanted to visit with his mother and whose poetry and literature were familiar to him since his childhood days.

I think therefore that his image, captured by different photographers, "will appear to be very happy" because the light of his star will shine in the City of Lights that he always so admired.

Alberto Granado
La Havana, 1 December 2002

Pero existe en este hombre extraordinario, otro tipo de sensibilidad que solo el contacto, directo y continuado con él permitía descubrir y era la sensibilidad para separar lo bello de lo feo, y lo diferente de lo común en el medio que lo rodeaba. Esta faceta de la personalidad del futuro Ché se pone de manifiesto en su gusto por la fotografía, que permite plasmar estas diferencias, placer estético que lo acompaña aun hoy cuando se ha transformado en el paradigma del hombre que hará posible la derrota del Capitalismo que hoy trata de globalizar la desigualdad, la miseria y la pérdida de los valores éticos.

Por último digamos que esta sensibilidad le permitió compenetrarse, muchas veces a través de la fotografía, en la cultura de países como Francia que siempre deseó visitar en compañía de su madre, y cuya poesía literatura conoció desde niño.

Considero por lo tanto, que su efigie captada por diferentes artistas del lente, está muy feliz, sabiendo que la luz de su estrella, brilla en la ciudad luz que tanto admiró.

Alberto Granado

La Habana 1º de Diciembre del 2002

3

REPUBLICA DE CUBA
MINISTERIO DE DEFENSA NACIONAL
EJERCITO

Departamento Militar de La Cabaña.
La Habana, 11 Marzo de 1959.

Mial:

No por esperada, tu carta me resultó menos agradable.
No te escribí, invitándote a esta mi nueva patria porque pensaba ir con Fidel a Venezuela. Acontecimientos posteriores me
impidieron hacerlo, pensaba ir un poco después y una enferme-
dad me retiene en cama. Espero poder ir dentro de un mes apro-
ximadamente.

Tan presente estaban ustedes en mi pensamiento que --
exigí cuando me invitaron a visitar a Venezuela, un par de
días libres para pasarlo con ustedes. Espero que pronto sean
estos deseos realidades; no te contesto tu filosofía barata de
la carta porque para eso hace falta un par de mates, una em-
panadita y algún rincón a la sombra de un árbol; allí charla-
mos.

Recibes el más fuerte abrazo que la dignidad de machi-
to te permita recibir de un idem.

Che

4

El "Che" estudiante de medicina y su amigo el Dr. Granados en el río Amazonas a la salida del leproso
río peruano de San Pablo en la balsa Mambo-Tango el 20 de Junio de 1952.

5

6

7

RIO AUSTRAL" - Temuco. martes 19 de febrero

2 expertos argentinos en leprología
recorren Sudamérica en motocicleta

Están en Temuco y desean visitar Rapa-Nui

DR. A. GRANADOS Y EL ESTUDIANTE E. GUEVARA
El raid llegará hasta la capital venezolana.

8   9

© Saúl Corrales

Jean Cormier Eyheraguibel
Born January 25, 1943 in Paris
Reporter for *Le Parisien* where he has been working
since he was 22 years old. Of Spanish heritage,
from the Basque region, he has undertaken more
than 70 trips to Latin America (22 to Cuba and 38
to Brazil); he speaks English as well as Spanish and
Portuguese. His Basque family lives in Rosario,
Argentina where Che was born. He is a rugby
specialist, a sport which links him to Che who played
for Cordoba, then Buenos Aires. Biographer of Che,
he researched his life for 8 years in his book *Che
Guevara* (Editions du Rocher). He is also the author
of *Che Compagnon de la Revolution* (Gallimard,
Collections Découvertes). He has produced three
documentaries on Che; the first one in 1987 with
Pierre Richard : *Parlez-moi du Che...* He is also
the director of a photography exposition celebrating
the 75th birthday of Che with exhibits in Paris, La
Rochelle and Bayonne, France and a final exposition
in Havana (end of 2003). This exhibition, dedicated
to Hildita, Che's oldest daughter who died the 21st
of August 1995, exhibits photographs taken by
photographers of the *Revolución*.

jean
cormier

THE MAGIC OF CHE PASSED THROUGH HERE!

This photo album is a history of brotherhood, of passion, of fervor, and of talent of which the men in question abound. It is an ancient history that joins the "Big History", that of Che Guevara and of the Cuban Revolution, which serves as a bridge between youth and the past. This youth which, in the beginning of this new millennium, is groping along on our "little ball" we call Earth that continues to witness everything between the moon that discreetly illuminates it at night and the sun, first witness of the defects of globalisation enhancing the inequities that flood the light of day. Light so dear to photographers that had their glory before the advent of television invaded the planet. And which conserves a privileged place : a film being a series of photos end to end, a photograph remains a very precise piece of history, the most accurate that exists. An image that sets off, in the spectator's head, a film that he makes up himself.

Photographers represent a race apart. They are journalists, yes, but not like the others. The writer can let himself hem and haw, he can bypass, skirt around, avoid, play with his subject; the photographer, he gives the absolute truth, crude, clean, dirty, as it is, with a cry of joy, of horror or of pleasure. The "presse-bouton" or photographer and the "gratte papier" or journalist form the two parts of the body of a trade that join together to make one; they are total complements.

As a chief reporter, I am used to working with photographers and also of interviewing them as was the case for Roger Pic, a giant of the profession who died the 3rd of December 2001 in Paris. He became a friend and participated in the August 1995 festival held for the launching of my biography of Che, in Basque country, in the village of Bunus in the middle of a corn field at the foot of the Pyrenees. Immense kakémonos displaying portraits of Che floated on the walls of an austere country house whose owner, Jean-Luc Berho, presided over an association for children with special needs. We ate some taloak (corn cakes) "à la ventreche" (type of lard eaten in Basque country), drank cider and listened to Imanol (a famous Basque singer) sing in "euskera" his monotonous chants that glorified the Basque culture. In this happy country setting, we began singing the song of Carlos Puebla's "Comandante"...

As much for modesty as for economic worries, the photographer that was Ernesto Guevara de la Serna known as Che, avoided being the line of sight of those image hunters of the *Revolución* who, attracted by his charisma, couldn't stop from following him. Obsessed with sharing, he considered, as ex-Minister of Finance, that expenses, no matter how small, were a waste. And according to him, to take and use even a miniscule piece of film in order to record his features was an insult to the Revolutionary spirit where equality should prevail up to the smallest details. Full of humor, even more of love, Che who incarnated his own words "To harden oneself without losing tenderness", did not joke with rigour.

Nevertheless, when one thinks about it, we are forced to recognize that without the photographers of the *Revolución*, he would not have such fame today, more than 35 years after his assassination (the 9th of October 1967 in La Higuera, Bolivia); and this, principally amongst the youth of a world that our passionate Pre-Columbian cultures called the "Pachamama", the Mother Earth of Incas "en quechua" (in the language of the Incas). The Cuban photographers which we are talking about are Chinolope, Raúl Corrales, Liborio Noval, Perfecto Romero, Salas Osvaldo and his son Roberto Osvaldo and also José Figueroa who worked on this "myth". Without forgetting, of course, Alberto Diaz known as Korda, author of the famous photo that the legend of Che transformed into an icon as much as the icon itself maintained it, held it up and accelerated the process of the myth. It is also necessary to call upon the presence of the Swiss photographer, René Burri, based in Paris and of Roger Pic, wonderful and dear Roger who died around the time of the exposition "Les

THE MAGIC OF CHE PA

Chemins du Partage", in La Rochelle, where he had invited Raúl Corrales to present his images of Che communicating his humanism with a sunny smile. Humanism with a capital H as big as the rugby goals of his childhood in Cordoba in the Cordillère, on the Argentinian slopes.

Ernesto Guevara would have surely detested all of this rubbish, this pile of accumulated photos to his glory but, because of this tribute on the occasion of the 75th anniversary of his birth (the 14th of June 1928 in Rosario, Argentina), we are not hesitating to drive the nail in by making a Christ Guerillero that the Andins call with veneration San Ernesto de la Higuera, the standard bearer of a more just world. Che repeated that among men brother will turn against brother; it is for this reason that he attempted to recreate the world. In vain one could say. No, certainly not for the photographs of the Revolution that affirm that Che is not far away, only a small flame in the big furnace that he had wished to light up to recreate several Viet Nams, these famous "focos" (places where there is fire) of South America, subsist in those who thought that his combat of Simon Bolivar in modern times was not in vain. "Che is not dead, he still lives…" they sing together as if they were singing the refrain from a new song. Because "his" photographers wished it, neither in this book nor in the accompanying exhibition, appear photos of Che kneeling, his body riddled with the bullets from the Bolivian lieutenant who had to get totally drunk in order to find the courage to execute the order to kill him.

When, with the photo-journalist Philippe Séclier (responsible for the photos linked to the Pachamama association) we left Orly for Havana, filled with fervor at the idea of meeting the creators of the image of Che, these "unseen" architects that pushed their target into the limelight, we no longer knew what equipment we would have to bring in order to construct our "guévarienne" expo. It was true that I knew Diana, the heriditary daughter of Korda, Raúl Corrales, the twin of Korda's dark rooms, Liborio Noval to

whom I introduced myself during an exhibition in Paris, as well as José Alberto Figuerioa, Korda's disciple, whom I regularly saw next to him; but missing were the others : Robert Salas, Romero and Chinolope. Chinolope, I must admit, particularly intrigued me. To help us in our desire to approach these "Masters" of the photograph, we could count on Alberto Granado, "El Petiso" , a brilliant little man with a big heart who, as soon as something concerns Che, becomes totally available, a friend for life of Ernesto Guevara de la Serna with whom he shared the taste for reading and the passion for sports. In the Miramar quarter that harboured the old glories of the *Revolución*, el Petiso, who has lived over 80 springtimes, put away his golf clubs to take out his old, dusty books. With his love of friendship and his love of celebrations, he spent an evening strengthening the ties between the photographers of his adopted country – one must remember that he is from Argentina as was Che.

Since our photography friends asked me to talk about my meetings with them in a narrative which was to serve as the connecting thread running through this book, I invite you to come back with me to the genesis of my Guévarienne adventure that permitted me to put together a biography of Che with Editions du Rocher, a book in the Decouvertes collection chez Gallimard and in three documentary films.

My Basque origins and the fact that a branch of my family, the Eyheraguibel, continues to proliferate in Rosario, the city where Che first saw the light of day, count as several of the magnets that pulled me toward the trail of the South American revolutionary. Without Una Liutkus, a Lithuanian in Paris, a sort of bridge between France and Cuba who gave so much to permit the French to discover the green Caiman Islands and its glorious history, these words would probably not appear before us today. In 1967, he offered his time to do volunteer work before marrying the actress Mirta Ibarra (appearing in Tomas Gutierrez Aleas's film *Strawberry and Chocolate*). He cubanised himself to the point of becoming

Philippe Séclier, Jean Cormier, Saúl Corrales et Carlos Torres Cairo during their meeting about the realisation of this book.

Liborio, Cormier, Séclier, Granado, Corrales, Salitas, Figueroa, at Granado's house to discuss the project concerning this book.

the second ambassador of the *Revolución* in the country of the Revolution of 1789, in a quite peaceful manner, through the bias of tourism, as director of Havanatour.

...I met Norka, the "guerrillera", in Paris at the end of the sixties at the house of one of my friends at that time, Lulette Bechet, who was the daughter of General Bechet. I was partying with Lulette and sleeping with the General. Two pages of *Paris Match* were dedicated to Norka, one where she appeared in an olive green uniform with her rifle, her look angry; the other where she posed as a model with Dior, slender, sublime, with wide open eyes, gothic flamboyant. With, on the night stand in the small apartment, a bullet from Che's cartridge that Che had given her when they briefly met in Havana in the trimphant aftermath of the *Revolución*. Thus, Che was already knocking at the door of my heart and my spirit!! Then, in September 1981, I took off for Havana with two signed letters of Lulette's. One for Norka, the other for Korda, her ex-husband. One must realise that Korda and I had the same inclination for the bottle and also, why hide it, for beautiful women. Even if I had not yet read *Alcools de Nuit* with Antoine Blondin and Roger Bastide, my close brothers of the confederation of the "Leveuers de Coude", if asked to choose between drinking and driving, I have already chosen, since the sexagenarian that I am still does not have a driver's license.

While explaining how to master the strong caress of "ron" (rum), Alberto Diaz known as Korda told me how he immortalised Che for eternity on paper, the 5th of March 1960,

the photo which appeared foremost in the journal *Revolución* and taken just after the explosion of the French cargo ship "La Coubre", full of Belgian arms, where almost 100 died in the port of Havana. This attempted attack attributed to the CIA marked the beginning of the destruction of the bond with the United States and led to the embargo of the island during the Cuban Missile Crisis of October 1962 where the ironmen Kennedy/Khrustchev almost caused a nuclear war. At the corner of 23rd and 12th streets, on the platform where once were Jean-Paul Sartre and Simon de Beauvoir, close to the Colon cemetary in order to permit the Cuban leaders to give tribute to those who have disappeared, Fidel spoke for the first time the historic words "Patria o muerte, venceremos!". And Korda recalls in the documentary *Parlez-moi du Che*, produced with Pierre Richard, who by the way is called the zapata negro in all of Cuba because of his film *Le Grand Blanc avec une Chaussure Noir* (*The Tall Blond Man with One Black Shoe*) : "After having taken the portrait of President Dorticos and of Fidel, there was an emptiness. I didn't raise my head. I only moved my Leica 1 with a 90 millimeter objective. And there appeared the hard, terrible, accusing face of Che. His expression was so "impressive" that my reaction was to back up, but in the same second, I clicked on the button... It is The Photo..." The Picture !! Raúl Corrales, the old friend, would receive it much later, in the 80s, with a dedication, part wink and part tribute kiddingly "giving him the finger", "This photo, I know that you could have taken it, but I screwed you!!"

"After having taken the portrait of President Dorticos and of Fidel, there was an emptiness. I didn't raise my head. I only moved my Leica 1 with a 90 millimeter objective. And there appeared the hard, terrible, accusing face of Che. His expression was so "impressive" that my reaction was to back up, but in the same second, I clicked on the button… It is The Photo…"

© Jose A. Figueroa

Alberto Diaz known as Korda
Born September 14, 1928, died May 25, 2001 in Paris.
1946-47. Commercial studies, Candler College, Havana.
1959-62. Photographer for the journal *Revolución*.
1959-63. Accompanies Fidel Castro on his trips.
1961. Founding member of the photography department of the "Union of Cuban Writers and Artists" (UNEAC).
1968-80. Photographer for the Department of "Investigaciones Submarinas" (scuba diving) of the Academy of Sciences.
1980-82. Director of the photography review *Opina*.

alberto
korda

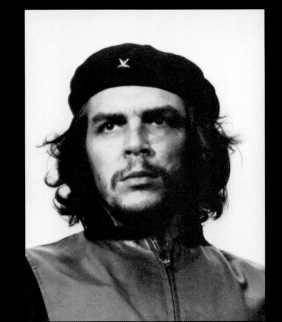

12

13   14

16

17

18

19

20

21

21

5 peso note signed by Che when he was President of the National Bank of Cuba.

One fine evening, with a rosy sun showing over the *Malecón* and sprays of salty water lashing at daring children, Korda baited me in a marine bar in a port called *Los dos hermanos* by asking me "You want to meet Che's father?" A lure that had the effect of a tidal wave on me. And thus embarked the visitor, heart slung across his shoulder, in a vagabond mood... The smell of rum invading the inside of the car, the Lada took the seaside road up to the house of Ernesto Guevara's father in the Miramar quarter. There, in a setting of Argentinian green with flowers swaying like hands in movement as if agitated by the wind of history written by his son, we were invited to taste a quantity of mojitos. We spoke about rugby, a passion that we shared. Remembering that it is precisely "El Petiso", Alberto Granado, who taught Che how to play rugby in Cordoba, with his rugby nickname as Fuser, from Furibondo (the Furibond) and la Serna (his mother's name). He told me that in crucial moments during the guerilla war, rugby was very useful for Che, for its altruistic values, for the self-denial that it fostered and also for the respect of elaborate tactics. After about 4 hours of semi-monologue – I drank his words with even more delectation than I drank those mojitos - he assured me that one of these days Che would come and help the Pachamama to liberate themselves from imperialism in all of its forms.

It was a telluric meeting that transformed itself in a mind-blowing way : my life as a wandering soul was going to change its course or moreso anchor itself in Cuba. I would return there more than 20 times. Always on Che's trail. Never forgetting to salute my Havanise tutor Korda in his lair in La Puntilla, between the Vedado and Miramar quarters at the mouth of the Almendares River where his elderly mother watched resignedy over her charming and boulimic son who burned the candle at both ends.

A man of the seaside, Korda was a special kind of sailor. Much like a sailor, he lived on high tides, drank lots of "ron", old "ron", the color of amber like the derrieres of "metissé" mixed race models that posed for him. In June 2001, he left Paris for the "Grand Ailleurs", the "Great Out There", two days after our dinner at the Neo-Café in Saint Germain des Prés where he sat in a chair with a cigar in one hand and an "anejo" aged 7 years in the other. His spirit soared in the curls of smoke of one and in the sensual delight of the other. Signed Korda!

Thanks to him, I met the colourful Raúl Corrales with whom we had the pleasure of spending lots of time in La Rochelle in November 2001 in the company of his alter ego Roger Pic; they were as thick as thieves together. The caustic humor and the surly tenderness of Korda, the pacific brother-in-arms, seduced the world of artists, painters, sculptors and sketchers also invited to La Rochelle-La Rebelle.

If the occasion presents itself, go by Cojimar where the Corrales live; don't miss it!! Cojimar is a fishing village where in December 2001, Gregorio Fuentes died at the age of 101; he was the captain of the yacht "Pilar" that belonged to Ernest Hemingway. There in a house built in the 50s, he was born amongst huge American cars some of which have resisted time, 3 caged parakeets, 2 turtles and a bastard dog who watched over the place always ready to go crazy over the appearance of a surprise visitor. In the back of the kitchen, a Raúl Martinez painting occupies a major part of the wall. It's called "La Suerte" meaning "Chance" and represents Nixon and Kennedy over a pack of fortune-telling cards. "A premonition painting painted a short time before the assasination of Kennedy..." states Saúl Corrales, son of Raúl, who devoted much of himself and his time in the realisation of this book.

Raúl Martinez, as well known in Cuba as Wifredo Lam whose Afro-Cuban pieces marked Che who passed away in 1995 he received the national 1st prize in Plastic Arts in 1994. Two years younger than Raúl Corrales, his friend from Ciego de Ávila, he is the only photographer that received this distinction; a title of which he was very proud, while never showing it, like Le Senor!

Corrales' beginning as a photographer merits to be told. At 18 years of age, he cleaned hardwood floors at Le Cuba

Chinolope, Salitas, R. Corrales, Séclier and Liborio during their meeting at Granado's house.

Salitas, Figueroa and Liborio listening to Cormier as he explained the project concerning this book.

© Saúl Corral

© Saúl Corral

Sono Films, propaganda agency of the Cuban Communist Party called at that time, in 1941, "Partido Socialista Popular". One of the photographers for the photo agency, Paco Altuna, proposed to teach him the fundamentals of this trade. For this, Raúl woke at dawn to carry out his labour in order to discover the secrets of the "black box", the function of the Graphic Speed. One evening the boss barked out in the corridors in search of a photographer for a job : nenni, no one!! Young Raúl became bold and offered to lend his services. Rather than losing a client, the agency chief accepted since he had no other choice. The teenage novice appeared proud, jubilant with this responsibility in the streets of Havana with his equipment, camera, tripod,... He got looks from others and rather enjoyed this. He took the photo of the Jewish Tailors Festival and returned to the agency. When the big boss asked to see the negative, he gave him the photo already developed. "Starting tomorrow, you will no longer wash floors. You will be a photographer," said the boss.

After a filling lunch washed down with wine at the Corrales house, they proposed that we go to the Museum of Fine Arts in old Havana where the Lauriet of the Year would receive his award. Without having thought about it, we set off for Havana the same day that the artists (plastic arts) held their meeting; this is what I consider to be part of Che's magic. Everyone was there. With his photo-journalist vest with pockets everywhere, "he" was waiting at the top of the steps leading to the Museum, "he" is Chinolope, the author of the photo of "Commandante" that immensely moved me. Che raised the end of his nose with his right index finger seeming to ask, eyes lifted towards the sky, "Where is this world going to?". Chinolope, I have been looking for him almost 20 years. When I asked how to find him, all sorts of strange answers were given. Like, "he is in the hospital", "he no longer lives in Havana", "they say he's dead". One would think that they were trying to hide him.

He would confirm as truth the legend about his being near death in 1958 when, as a young boy, he tried his chance in New York and when Tatica, a musician who played the bongo drums, trumpet, and occasionally took photos, lent him his camera so that he could take several shots to sell to a New York magazine. Like this, Lopez wandered the streets of New York with Tatica's black box wrapped in a cloth. Hearing the bullets whistle by, he took refuge in a barbershop. There where the gangster José Anastasia got a shave just before the rival gang members shot him down. "They paid me lots for this photo" he told me standing there before me and looking much younger than his age. One would say he's 50, when he is well over 70. Sitting side by side, we attended the award ceremony where the painter Adigio Benitez received his prize before going back to his place in the Marianao quarter not far from the Tropicana, the famous and legendary "dance hall and cabaret". Chinolope's habitation is surprising by its rusticness. One gets there, as is often the case in Havana, via a narrow passage between 2 blocks of houses. Esperanza, his lawyer wife, lived in France and is an expert in the language of Moliere. His real name, Guillermo Fernandez Lopez; the extravagent person that he is, too dignified to be living in such a house, specifies, "It's Che who gave me the name Chinolope. From Chino because of my Asian features and Lopez from Lopez in my name. I am very stubborn and Che knew it when at the University of Havana in 1959, the year of victory in the revolution, he refused to have his photo taken,... He was surrounded by students, a milieu that he particularly appreciated. After having snubbed me and letting me understand that he didn't want me to click on the shutter, I insisted to the point of driving him crazy. And suddenly, he took this pose where he raised his nose up slightly as if in this thinking pose, trying to make a decision. It was the perfect photo!" Photo that Che's family are proud of; this gesture where he slightly raises his nose is really a family mannerism meaning something like "let me think!" Here, Esperanza rallys those who think that this image of Che interrogating should join the ranks of or even replace Rodin's "The Thinker".

23

I am not a friend of Che; I worked with him.

In 1959, I was the Director of Photography at the INRA (National Institute of Agrarian Reform). Che, as Director of Industries of the INRA, organized a meeting one day in his office where he showed us *Life Magazine* and told us that the next edition of the INRA review would also be like this, entirely in colour. This was how we began to work on each edition and he personally indicated to us the themes and subjects to work on. Then we would decide together the photos that we would use. There still exists old editions of these reviews, still in perfect condition after more than 44 years. On September 14th, 1959, Che was on TV for the first time since his nomination to the post of Director of Industries of the INRA. I was in the television studios and shot several rolls of film from a certain distance with my Nikon SP and a 35mm teleobjective. I chose several of these portraits, printed them on 8x10 paper, then put them in an envelope and placed them in his office and left. A half hour later he came into my office, gave me back my photos and said, "The photos are good, it's you that's not good. Why and for what reason did you take so many photos of me? You have to learn not to waste the resources of the country. Don't be an apple polisher!" He turned around and left.

I was a photographer for a long time and I have continued to take photos of many "personalities". But I have never ever again given my photos away to anyone.

Raúl Corrales

24

© Philippe Séclier

Raúl Corral known as Corrales
Born January 29, 1925 in Ciego de Ávila. Lives in Cojimar near Havana.
1957-59. Studies Graphic Art and journalism student at the school "Manuel Marquez Sterling" in Havana.
1944-46. Lab and photo assistant at *La Cuba Sono Films Habana*.
1953-54. Collaborates as a photographer for Fidel Castro.
1959-61. Accompanies Fidel Castro as his photographer.
1959-62. Photographer for the journal *Revolución*.
1961.Founding member of the Photography Department of the Union of Cuban Writers and Artists (UNEAC).
1962-73. Chief of the "Central Department of Photography of the Academy of Science".
1964-91. Chief of the microfilms and photography section that he created.

c o r r a l e s

22

23

24

28

25

26

27

31

32

33

When things impose on us their principle of reality, a photograph is only a "temporal and spatial" way of attaining a goal: The imaginative eye permits us to live in conformity with the pressures of society. All other senses are subordinate to the life that is drowning itself and escaping itself, the life that made it. Photography perceives what the thinking is hiding, something like a costume that hides from us the mobility of things as soon as they appear without realizing that they only represent silent metaphors.

"To Che….this here is my spirit when it touches and grasps the sadness of death….this here is my tribute to him and to all photographers all over the world."

Chinolope

34

© Philippe Séclier

Chinolope
From his real name Guillermo Fernando López. Born the 10th of February 1932 in Havana where he lives.
1959. Photographer for the journal *Revolución*.
1961. Founding member of the Photography Department of the Union of Cuban Writers and Artists (UNEAC).
1984. Photographer for the review *El Caiman Barbudo*.
The intellectual of the group that worked with Jean-Luc Godard and produced the photo of Che with the look "as if he was interrogating the stars" on his face.

c h i n o l o p e

al Che... esta espíritu cuando troca y alcanza su tristeza de muerte... esta es mi dedicatoria a él y a todos los fotógrafos del mundo...

chimuelope

Cuando   los   hechos   nos   imponen   su
principio de la   realidad, el fotógrafo
no es sino una   oportunidad de tiempo y
lugar para hacer   o conseguir algo: el
ojo de la imaginación nos permite vivir
de acuerdo con   las presiones del medio
y todo   otro sentido se   subordina a la
vida que   fluye y que escapa   a la vida
que lo ha creado.   La fotografía ve lo
que   el pensamiento oculta: sería algo
así   como   un enmascaramiento   que   nos
oculta la movilidad de las cosas, desde
el momento en que son, sin darse cuenta
de   que   son   tan   sólo   metáforas
silenciosas.

36

10 peso note signed by Che when he was President of the National Bank of Cuba.

For certain of his photography colleagues, Chinolope is an intellectual who has marginalized himself because of his overactive mind, always brainstorming, always "racking his brains". In 1965,In 1965, he spent time with Jean-Luc Godard with whom he worked in Havana on video-reality : "Godard often told us that cinema is the truth in 24 images a second", reminises the Chinese Lopez. Che's magic in operation, he trusted us with the negative of his photo. One knows how much a negative is sacred for a photographer, it's the essense of his life. "Without confidence, one doesn't do much!! In the beginning of his "act", a photographer is less an artist than a discoverer. And then comes the idea that the best way of being original is precisely not to have any desire to be," contently said by the man. Eusebio Leal Spengler, the restaurant owner of old Havana said about this "with the mastery of this art, Chinolope faithfully illustrated the strong conviction renown by the Indian South American who believed that a part of the soul of a person remains a prisoner when their photo is taken." This just vision of things could explain itself by a phrase of Che's that had marked "El Chino" : "Work is a gift, not a piece of merchandise that is sold."

Then we couldn't wait to go to Liborio Norel's place in the popular Vedado quarter. An apartment from the period when Europe was at war, a haven of peace where everything is arranged with taste and precision, like the images of his contact sheets, Liberio presents himself as a disciple and student of Raúl Corrales, 9 years older than him, both born the 29th of January under the sign of Aquarius, the first in 1934, the second in 1925. For a long time official photographer of Fidel during his trips, Liberio, now retired, began to work for the journal *Revolución* before lending his services to Granma, the paper that was, starting in 1965, the organ of the party. Puffing with delectation some tobacco that was fogging up his eyeglasses, he remembers, "the 29th of January 1964, day of the celebration of the fifth birthday of the triumph of the Revolution at the place called just that "Revolution Plaza" , I was working for the journal

Revolución, Oh yes!! With my Soviet "Star" camera with a 300mm telephoto lens. Che made me come and stand on the tribune so he could ask me what kind of camera I was using. I explained to him, he looked at it, used it and gave it back to me before telling me that one day he would be asking me to borrow it. I seized the occasion to take several photos of him. Then, when I looked at the photos when developed, I saw that Che had taken several photos of Fidel,…"

In the crowd, I saluted Alberte Juantorena, the 2nd Cheval of the Island, the first was Fidel Castro, known as "el Caballo" (Spanish for horse). Juantorena is the holder of the one and only double 400 meter, 800 meter record in the history of the 1976 Olympics held in Montreal where he hastily offered his medals to Fidel and to the Revolution. This leads us to Che, asmathic, who shouted strongly at the top of his voice until out of breath and trained himself to surpass himself in practicing numerous sports before covering, as a photographer, the PanAm Games of 1955 in Mexico. Even today in Havana, all is done to incite one to become infatuated with Che, as if the mangrove woven by the 82 "invaders" of Granma that would debark the 2nd of December 1956 on the oriental coast had transformed itself into an invisible cover, enticing and bringing together these visitors that were the soul of the leftists, potentially "guévarists", when they landed on the island that sealed the destiny of the "Comandante. Everywhere in Cuba, the portraits of Che, mocked at by the indecency of the God dollar, attempting to preserve the spirit of the *Revolución*…

In Paris, during an exposition organised by La FNAC – not the Forces Nationales Antichars (Anti-tanks), but the Federation National des Acheteurs (Buyers) Cadres – in the belly of Paris, more exactly at the metro station Les Halles, I had approached Liberio Noval. Available, smiling, smoking, he talked of Korda who died in the same City of Lights. The next day we found each other again with Diana Diaz, Korda's daughter, in the hall of a hotel near an elevated metro station not far from the Cuban Embassy, in order to discuss the expo

of Che. On to the Montparnasse Museum, Roger Pic's base, another photographer who had shot Che, helping him also to become part of the collective imagination. Having learned that this historic place was preserved from being demolished by bulldozers because of the determination and tenacity of Picos – nickname given to Roger Pic by those close to him – Diane was sensitive of the light that fell from the windows and lit up the rooms where Che would be honored. Roger Pic who appreciated the modesty of Che and adapted himself to his "uncompromising excess", would have loved so much for Che to have used his Leica. Nevertheless, he would content himself with the photo that Guevara would take with another camera and which would symbolize Che as a photographer.

If they tease each other, sometimes rather scathingly and at times quite hard on each other, the photographers support and defend each other whenever one of them is attacked or criticized. We are not sure that the photographers of the revolution were always ready to trade a hammack for a walk in the Sierra Maestra but when it was in order to do something together for Che, well then, they stood up together as one. Yes, always the magic of Che!! To unit for his 75th birthday. To unite to glorify him in Paris, in La Rochelle-la-Rebelle and then in Bayonne-l'Euskarienne, in order to remind him that he had Basque blood in his veins. One couldn't have dreamt better than to put finishing touches on 2003 in the Phototech of the Plaza Vieja in Old Havana , created by the intermixing of races coming from an ocean that pigheadily hits its head on the *Malecón* like the tam-tam of a time that never ages!! For the "guajiros", peasants from the Sierre Maestra that he educated, Che, with his Argentinian accent so evident,

came from another place : the country of Peron, of Carlos Gardel, of the Utopia and of tango, of the "pampas", the grass-covered plains of Martin Fierro, of Salta, the city of General Güernes, his guerrilla master. The new Simon Bolivar who, as President of the National Bank, would sign the paper money "Che", son of Celia and Ernesto Guevara; this citizen of the world counted on education in order to raise the man to a state of true responsibility. On the documents of our photographer friends of the *Revolución*, numerous illiterate peasants that Le Che taught to read and to write are recognized, authenticating Cuban history, and made better by a doctor who understood how much education could eradicate a sickness called misery.

Salas, here's a name that resounds true when we walk in the footsteps of the photographers of Che. Osvaldo, the father, and Roberto, the son. The old man who is no longer with us here on earth since the 4th of May 1992, remains as El Viejo Salas, the youngest was known as Salitas. El Viejo, for whom the word friendship was sacred, was the soul of the group. He would not hesitate to offer an autographed baseball bat of a crack American player to a child who needed it. His photo of Che – profile photo where Che is smoking a cigar – taken the 26th of July 1964 in La Moncada, the famous barracks in Santiago from where everything began in 1953, has gone around the world. Since a long time, he has passed the lead to Salitas who lives with his family in a clean apartment inside a skyscraper, not far from the place where Korda shot "The Photo". Having left New York in his father's suitcases at the age of 19, he wasn't even 20 when he took the plane of his destiny on flight...

In 1960, I had already taken Che's photo several times under different circumstances, but it was only on the 26th of February 1961 that I spoke to him for the first time. I was working as a photographer for the journal *Revolución* and they sent me on this particular day, it was a Sunday, to cover some volunteer work in the Marti quarter where they were building houses for the poor who lived in the slums. When Che arrived, he asked me what I was doing there. I told him that I was sent to take some photographs for the magazine and he said he simply wanted to know if I came there to work. I answered in the affirmative because I was indeed there for the purpose of taking photos : that was my work.

He then asked me if I was able to work as a volunteer to help build houses. I told him "yes" and he told me, "Leave your camera here and come with me." This was how we came to work together. It was the first volunteer work for Che as Minister of Industries; in actuality, he had just taken up this job as Minister. He had the habit of doing volunteer work on Sundays ever since he decided to help build the Camilo Cienfuegos School situated on the slopes of the Sierra Maestra.

From then on, the journal began sending me more and more often to cover Che's "work". Ernesto sometimes talked to me about photography, what kind of film we were using. If it happened to be during the week, he would propose that we see each other the coming Sunday. We therefore began working together on various volunteer projects during his stay in Cuba. Until the day when he asked me to stop taking photos during the volunteer work. Intrigued, I asked him what had happened and he replied that there was nothing wrong with me, but as he was the only Minister to appear in the journal every Monday and always in photos where he was doing volunteer work on the Sunday, the other Ministers, during the Council Meetings would kid him and make jokes about it. It was therefore necessary to stop taking photographs; but I, on my side, was to continue doing the volunteer work.

On the 2nd of February 1964 during the celebration for the 5th Anniversary of the triumphant revolution, in Revolution Plaza in Havana, during a massive assembly, I was carrying my Soviet "Star" camera with a 300mm telephoto lens which was quite big. Che sent somebody to look for me and when I went up to the tribune, he began asking me about the camera I was using. After telling him, he took it, examined it's functions, looked at it for a short while and then told me that one day he would be borrowing it from me. I took advantage of the situation to take a few photos of him up close. When the film was developed, I saw that Che had taken Fidel's photo several times.

Liborio Noval

Liborio Noval
Born the 29th of January 1934 in Havana.
1953-1960. Photographer and representative for the advertising firm *Siboney*.
1959 - 65. Collaborates for the journal *Revolución*.
1960. Collaborates for the review *INRA*.
1965. Collaborates for the journal *Granma*.
1990 - 2001. Accompanying photographer of Fidel Castro during his trips.

liborio

44

42

40

41

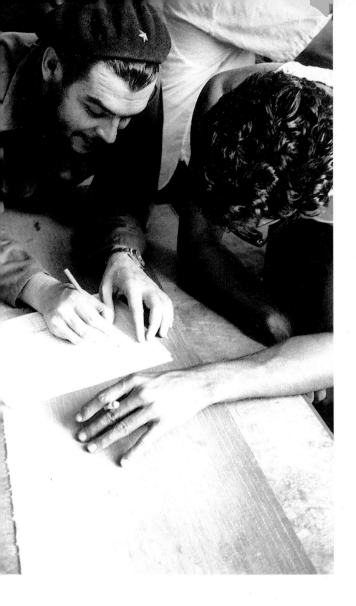

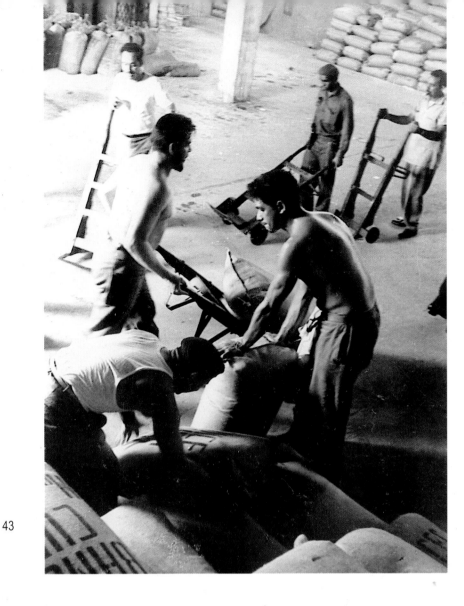

43

44

45

47

48

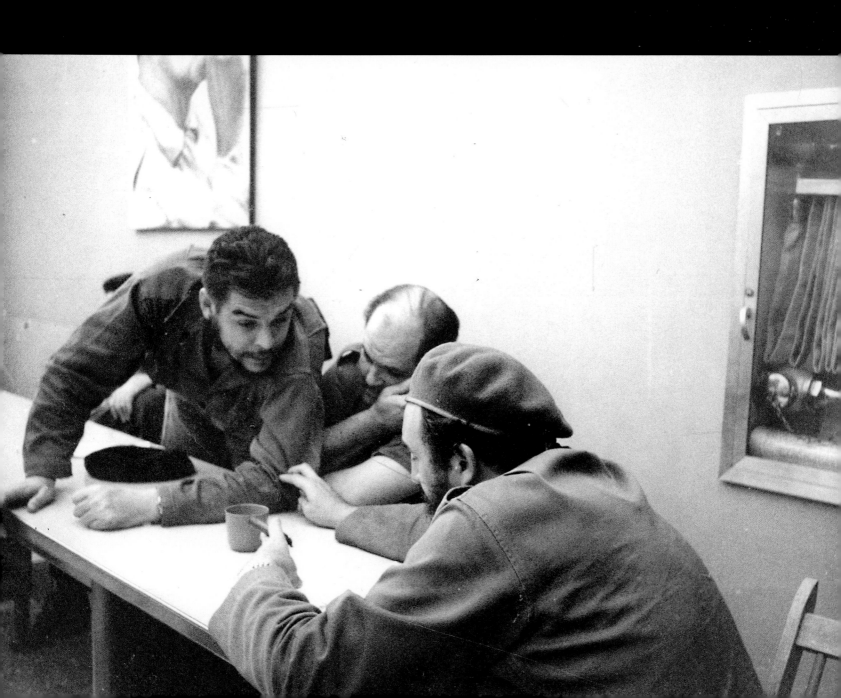

51

52

53

54

55

56

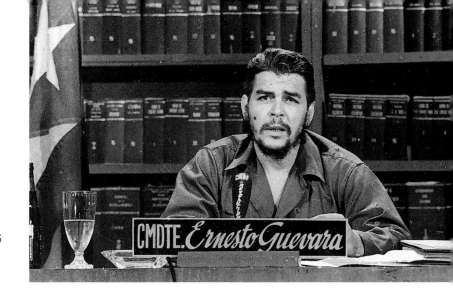

57

58

20 peso note signed by Che when he was President of the National Bank of Cuba.

In 1959, Manuel Urrutia, 1st President after the Cuban Revolution, left for New York with Fidel. A second plane was organised for the press. Still quite lively and clever, Korda was counted as one of the first on-board. A few seconds later arrives unexpectedly Raúl Corrales with Salas Jr. at his side. "The plane for the press is full, sorry!..." Corrales, whom we all knew was not afraid of anything, quickly advanced toward the President Urrutia : "You should know what is written on my passport..." And the photographer read : "Kindly ask the authorities to help the owner of this passport if any problems arise... You are indeed "el senor" Urrutia and thus the person who has signed this passport. So!....." The President indicated to Corrales that he could get on. Which he hurriedly did with Salitas sticking to him like glue. In the constant competition, friendly and stimulating, that the photographers had amongst each other, Korda had lost a point. The three colleagues laughed a long time over this presidential anecdote.

"When at the end of 1959 I returned to the Bronx, in New York where I was born in order to get my things and take them back to Havana where I was to continue living my life, I made the unfortunate discovery that thousands of my negatives had disappeared, probably because of the work of the FBI and the CIA. There were many photos of Che taken principally by my father who, it might be said, didn't want – he who had varicose veins – that I take up this career because having to stand a lot of the time is so painful and tiring!" Then, after having browsed through a small album full of nudes of a mulatto that he called Canela, Salitas affirmed : "The epoque of the Revolution has permitted us to change our work into art, in giving it an ethic force. To go from static photos with "les grandes chambres" (cameras used with the black veil against the light) to 35mm, to enjoying oneself immensely with different kinds of light, I call that a revolution. And, right in the middle of the Cuban Revolution makes it even better!"

Living in an austere house in Havana, Perfecto Romero Ramirez, debonair and good-natured with his bald, round head, was a member since 1955 of the Movement of 26 July 1953 that took place with the attack of the Moncada barracks by a group of insurgents led by Fidel Castro Ruz in Santiago de Cuba. He joined Che at El Pedrero in the mountains of L'Escambray during the invasion of "la columna ocho" in October 1958 for the final combat against the troops of Dictator Batista. El Pedrero, a place particularly memorable for Che as this is where he met his wife Aleida and found again his "brother in arms" Camilo Cienfuegos with his trademark cowboy hat and his dazzling smile, before the two leaders followed different roads to Havana, each leading his own group. "I rejoined Che with a group of youngsters from my village. When he learned that I knew how to take photos, he wanted to see my camera and asked me if I would become his war photographer and stipulated that he wished to have photos taken of the invasion in order to use them in the press, and that he would be in charge of finding a place to show them. I nevertheless kept my revolver, just in case. Che, who loved to chat about photography and different techniques, told me that his camera became waterlogged when he crossed a river and that it didn't work anymore. I saw him for the last time in April 1964, in La Rosita, in south Havana where he reunited "los Invasores", the liberators of the two columns, to spend a nice day of revolutionary friendship.

If nothing had changed in the sunny terraced apartment of José Alberto Figueroa Daniel, one now perceives stronger than before the fragrances of a past linked to Alberto Korda. From 1964 to 1968 his assistant in this "castriste" island, José Alberto sealed his destiny to that of his "helmsman". Playing with as much respect as with talent his masterpiece, the photo taken the 5th of March 1960. His room is like a small museum devoted to this "Master". Which proves how

"The Photographers" with Granado in the Emiliano Zapata Park on 5th Avenue, Havana.

Salitas taking photos of his colleagues with Séclier's camera.

© Saúl Corral

© Saúl Corral

much this quinquagenarian with the dark pupils was marked by "el senor" Alberto Diaz.

These "beautiful" people gathered in the villa that Fidel offered to Alberto Granado, offered not so much because he was Che's best friend, but because he aided the Revolution by researching and perfecting, primarily with this team of biologists, how one cow could give more milk than the others. For the current gathering there was a small piglet on the BBQ pit, skin turning a golden color. Accompanied by beer, some rum and also, for some of the people, some whiskey, it would satisfy these male photographers accompanied by their wives. Soon, jokes and teasing would take over. An evening of brotherhood and complicity where the sacred union for Che was so natural. And from there was born this album!

The next day, we reunited the group of 7 and took them to a nearby square named after the Mexican revolutionary Emiliano Zapata, to the foot of a colossal tree, what is called a "fromager" in French, that had roots which seemed to go up to the heavens. It was amusing and moving to see the six "ancient" photographers : Corrales, Noval, Salas, Romero, Chinolope and Figueroa pose around the unforgettable Granado who lent us some personal documents which included some photos of his youth with Che and some exchanges of letters. As the magic of Che would have it!

We then had 9 photographers, 8 Cubans and Roger Pic of which his children, Dominique and Frédéric, said with no hesitation a sound "yes" when asked if we could borrow the negatives of Che. Now we had to get our hands on the 10th person of the group, the Swiss René Burri, lifetime member of the Magnum agency, always on the go, the eternal voyager. Black hat and grey scarf, classy, charming in his Parisian studio in Belleville, Burri adhered with all his "guévarienne" fervor to the double idea of having an exposition as well as an album. He remembers : "It was in January 1963, 4 years after the triumph of the Revolution. I was accompanying, as photographer representing Magnum, a famous American journalist, Laura Bergquist from *Look Magazine* for her interview with Che who received us in his office at the Ministry of Industries. She asked him questions which made Che react strongly and who, cigar in his hand, showed this woman who represented the enemy, an incredible panoply of attitudes, all under complete and total control while defending ferociously the cause of the Revolution. In this collision of two conceptions from two different sides of the world, Che completely forgot me. This is how I was able to take 8 rolls of film...."

Intentions launched from the heights of the City of Lights, while drinking a bottle of "ron" to the memory of those no longer with us : Che, Osvaldo Salas, Korda and Pic... Oh yes, the magic of Che continues and will continue to act... Beginning with Paris where our Princes of film were invited to get together again and to celebrate the heathen mass of the revolutionary brotherhood in memory of an athiest photographer, unlike any other, by the name of Ernesto!!

Jean Cormier Eyheraguibel

"Salas, here's a name that resounds true when we walk in the foot-steps of the photographers of Che. Osvaldo, the father, and Roberto, the son. The old man who is no longer with us here on earth since the 4th of May 1992, remains as El Viejo Salas, the youngest was known as Salitas. El Viejo, for whom the word friendship was sacred, was the soul of the group. He would not hesitate to offer an autographed baseball bat of a crack American player to a child who needed it. His photo of Che – profile photo where Che is smoking a cigar – taken the 26th of July 1964 in El Moncada, the famous barracks in Santiago from where everything began in 1953, has gone around the world…"

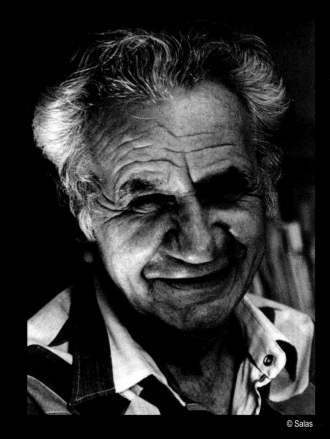

© Salas

Osvaldo Salas
Born the 29th of March 1914 in Havana where he died the 5th of May 1992. He lived in New York from 1926 to 1959. then in Havana from 1959 to 1992.
1947. Member of the Inwood Camera Club in New York.
1950 - 58. Collaborator for the journal *La Prensa* and for the review *Vision* in New York, *El Clarin* in Buenos Aires and to the Cuban review *Bohemia*.
1959 - 60. Collaborates with the journal *Revolución*.
1960 - 62. Chief of Photography department for the *Revolución*.
1961. Founding member of the Photography Department for the Union of Cuban Writers and Artists (UNEAC).
1965 to 86. Photo-reporter for the journal *Granma*.

o s v a l d o
s a l a s

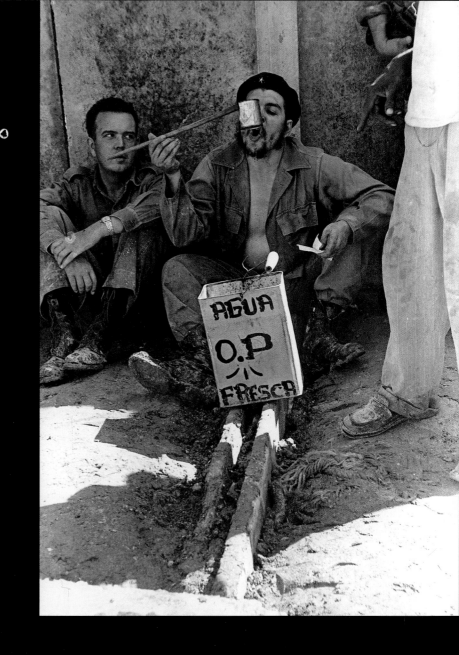

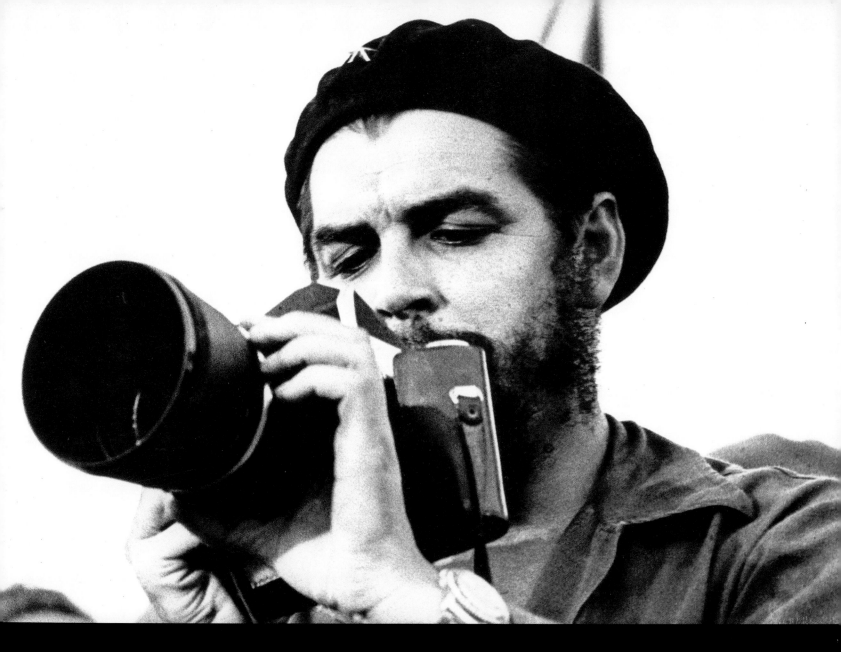

63

64

65

67

68

I could talk about many different things that I remember about the photos that we took of Che. Unfortunately, we didn't have so many chances to take his picture and I didn't have the intuition to take maximum advantage of my chances. Like everyone else, I thought he would always be there, that there would be many occasions and I always said to myself : "Whatever I don't do today, I can always do tomorrow." Che was with us for barely 5 years and if we look back, they were 5 short years of which a good part slipped away with diplomatic trips all around the world.

I will never forget the first time I took a photo of Che, not only because his presence was so overwhelming, but also because having taken a photo constitued a success in oneself, especially considering the conditions at the time. It was the second week after the revolutionary triumph of the 1st of January, in the ancient Presidential Palace of Batista at 3:30 AM. I had my small Leica 111F, I balanced myself on a big meeting room table that served as a tripod, and I took photos that I exposed either one, two or three seconds.

Another reason as to why I will never forget this photo is that its negative, along with another hundred or so negatives, were stolen from me by the CIA and the FBI in 1960 in New York. This affair was made known only two years ago when the FBI assumed responsibilty and declassified documents on this subject. Unfortunately, I lost my first photo of Che, but I will nevertheless never forget it.

Why didn't Che like it when we took his photo? I have a theory that is quite simple : do you know any photographer that likes having his photo taken? Don't forget that Che was also a photographer.

Roberto Salas

Roberto Salas known as Salitas
Born the 16th of November 1940 in the Bronx (New York), resides in Havana since 1959.
1956 - 57. Collaborates with the review *El Imparcial* and *Life magazine*, in New York.
1956 - 59. Collaborates with the journal *Sierra Maestra*, for *Organo del Movimiento 26 de Julio*.
1958 - 60. Photographer for the journal *Revolución*.
1961. Founding member of the Photography Department of the Union of Cuban Writers and Artists (UNEAC).
1962. Founding member of the Union of Cuban Journalists.
1962 - 67. Founding photographer of the journal *Granma*.
1965 - 67 and 1972 - 73. War correspondant in Viet Nam.

r o b e r t o
s a l a s

73

74

When Che arrived in Las Villas, in l'Escambray, the "Movimiento 26 de Julio" of Cabaiguan gave us the mission to reinforce the troops of the column "Ciro Redondo" by sending there a group of young from the 26th. In mid-October, we scrambled up the Gavilanes hills where we were to establish contact with Che and his companions.

After three days of walking, we fell upon the "scouts" of the column and, under an enormous bombing campaign, four "rebels" took us to Che. Around 5:00 PM, Che, sitting on a stool, received us one after the other. Those who weren't carrying any weapons were summoned to go back and get one.

When my turn arrived, he asked me where my weapon was. I told him that I didn't have one and he said to me, "You come to make war without a weapon?" Right then, his look fell upon my shoulder where I had my camera wrapped up and he asked me what it was. I told him that it was my camera and extended it out to him so that he could see it. He then began to tell me about the time when he was a photographer in Mexico : his camera became waterlogged during the invasion and someone proposed to repair it for him. He also explained to me the importance of having a group of correspondants in order to publish a journal in the mountains and gave me details of the necessary steps that he was in the process of undertaking in order to create a print shop for the purpose of publishing *El Cubano Libre*.

Che contacted his companion Olo Pantoja in order to find a place to build a photography laboratory. They sent me to Sancti Spiritus to buy everything I needed for developing photos, but given the lack of supplies during this time, I could only buy a few things. The war was accelerating, the soldiers weren't going out of their barracks and Che put in place the offensive against the tyranny of Batista. Cities and villages fell one after the other.

The one and only journal was written in Cabaiguan, but it had no photos, only written text.

This was how I knew Che.

Perfecto Romero

Perfecto Romero
Born the 25th of January 1936 in Cabaiguan
1955. Became photographer.
End of 1958. Participates as a war photographer in the combats of Fomento, Cabaiguan, Yaguajay and Santa Clara, also known as Che's city because it was he who took it from Bastista's troops.
1959. Photographer for the review *Verde Olivo*.
1960. Specialises in underwater photos.
1978. Accompanies Raul Castro in Algeria and in Angola.
1982. Accompanies Fidel Castro to Nicaragua.

perfecto
romero

76

77

79

80

81

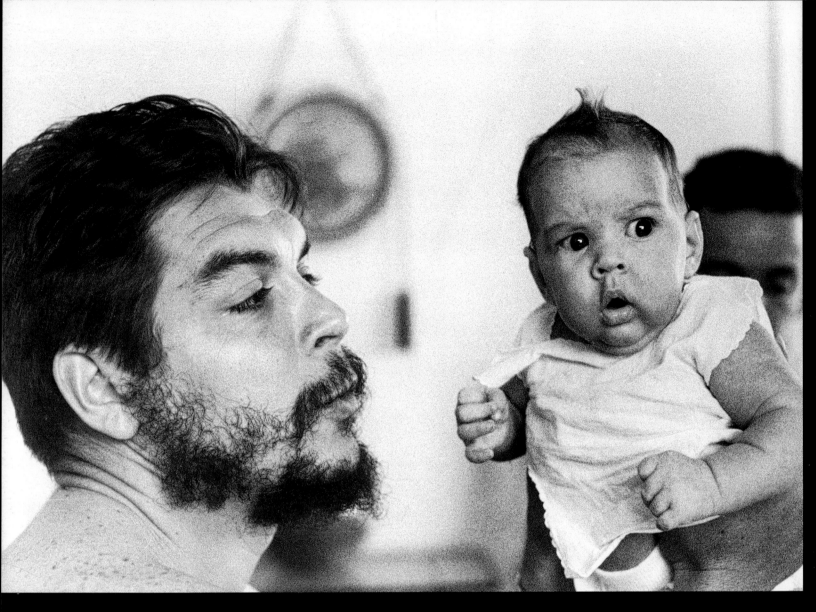

84

85

86

87

89

88

90 91

"Roger Pic, who appreciated the modesty of Che and adjusted himself to his uncompromising access, would have liked so much that the "Comandante" use his Leica. Nevertheless, he should content himself with the photo that Guevara would take with another camera and that would symbolise Che as a photographer."

Roger Pic

Born the 15th of September 1920 in Paris. Died the 3rd of December 2001 in Paris.

1939. Rents at 21, avenue du Maine, his first studio for taking care of his amateur theatre group.

1944. Returns to Paris after the resistance. Directs *Libido* with Boris Vian at the *Rose Rouge*.

1944. One of the creators of 'l'Association des photographes de presse" of which he became the general secretary.

1960. First voyage to China.

1962 .First voyage to Cuba, edition of two records of Cuban music that he taped.

1963. Photos of Che and Castro; television reports on the war in North Vietnam for *Cinq Colonnes à la Une*.

1966. Interviews Ho Chi Minh.

1972. Photographs and films Nixon's first visit to Peking

1988. In Africa films the documentary "Plaidoyer pour l'Afrique".

2000. Retrospective at the Chemin du Montparnasse for his 80th birthday.

r o g e r   p i c

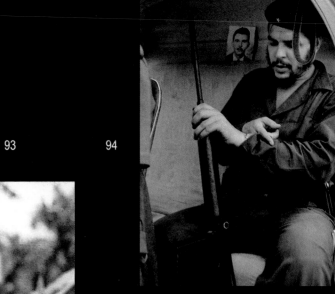

93

94

95

96

100

101

104

INSTITUTO CUBANO DEL ARTE E INDUSTRIA CINEMATOGRA

106

jornada del
guerrillero
heroico

105

octubre del 8 al 15
ORGANIZACION CONTINENTAL
LATINOAMERICANA DE ESTUDIANTES

JORNADA
DEL
GUERRILLERO
HEROICO
octubre 8 al 15 1969

l a g r

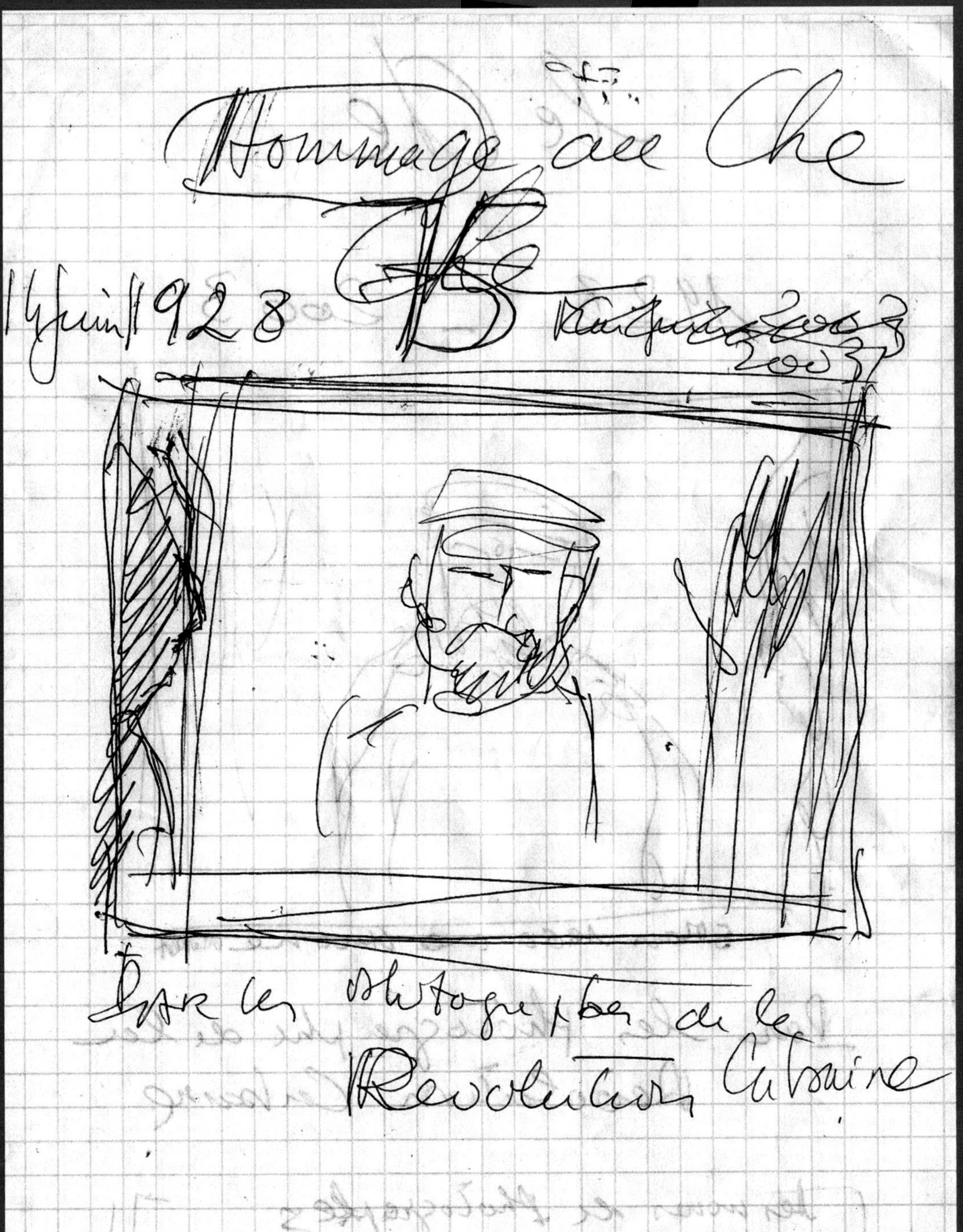

l a g r

15

El Primer Secretario del Partido Comunista de Cuba, comandante Fidel Castro, en los momentos en que daba lectura a la carta del compañero Ernesto Che Guevara.

Granma

Organo Oficial del Comité Central del Partido Comunista de Cuba

La Habana, Lunes 4 de octubre de 1965. Precio 5 centavos. Año 1 / Número 1

...mbros y los objetivos de n...

...CC ...no

Che: otras tierras reclaman mis modestos esfuerzos

Frente al doloroso hec...

113

6 *Granma* | La Carta de Che a Fidel

La Habana, Lunes 4 de Octubre de 1965

EN LOS NUEVOS CAMPOS DE BATALLA

q'vale la pena conocer
a ustillas. Hasta la victoria
siempre. Patria o Muerte

Te abraza con todo fervor
revolucionario,

Granma 7
La Habana, Lunes 4 de Octubre de 1965

LLEVARE LA FE QUE ME INCULCASTE

q'vale la pena conocer
a ustillas. Hasta la victoria
siempre. Patria o Muerte

Te abraza con todo fervor
revolucionario,

Havana 1963. It's a state of war between Cuba and the United States. Two years earlier was the failed assault attempt organised by John F Kennedy of the landing in the Bay of Pigs. One year earlier, the Cuban Missile Crisis almost provoqued the Third World War. At that time, as photographer for the *Magnum* agency, I accompanied the journalist Laura Bergquist for a meeting which, in its context, was literally extraordinary : it was in order to interview for *Look Magazine*, this wonderful representative of the great American press, the number two of the Cuban Revolution, Che Guevara. He received us in his office at the Ministry of Industries. Two hours of interviews, two hours of extremely tense confrontation. Not only did the journalist represent the detested Yankee enemy, but she practiced journalism in the American style with provoking questions : across from her, the man who represented in the eyes of the leaders of and in the opinions of the United States, was the man to destroy, even more than Fidel Castro, and who wasn't bad himself in giving provocative answers. It was the shocking encounter of two worldly conceptions, irreconcilable. During the interview, Che didn't pay attention to me and didn't pose. I used 8 rolls of film. Certain photos made and still make world news. Since that day, it seems that the image and the character of Che has never left me. This entire book is witness to all this. Much later, in 1987, when I returned to Havana, I photographed in the streets living signs of the presence of "Comandante", dead twenty years earlier. I find the photos exposed in the Museum of the Revolution are very much points of reference in the life of the guerilla : of the Sierra Maestra in the Cuban guerilla, of the Valle Grande in the Bolivian guerilla. I have also bought some right there in the streets. And later, I went to Bolivia and found the places where Che spent his last moments and for the book, I look in my own archives for photos that I took a while back during my trips to Latin America at the same spots where my footsteps had crossed with those of this young man who was not yet known as El Comandante Ernesto Che Guevara.
It is therefore the thread of a life that unwinds itself here, as seen by my eye and by that of my objective.

René Burri
Propos recueillis by François Maspero

94

© Carlos Torres Cairo

René Burri
Born the 9th of April 1933 in Zurich, Switzerland.
1948. Student at the School of Arts and Metiers in Zurich.
1955. Begins working at the *Magnum* agency.
1959. Reportage on the "gauchos des pampas" of Argentina, the homeland of Che.
1960. Photographs Picasso, Giacometti and Le Corbusier
1960 - 70 Reportage in Vietnam, Cambodia and Cuba.
1963.Trip to Cuba, photos of Fidel and a series of photos of Che smoking a cigar.

rené burri

115

115

40. Woche · Zinstage 276-84
Freitag
6
OKTOBER

OKTOBER 67   NOVEMBER 67

S	1	8	15	22
M	2	9	16	23
D	3	10	17	24
M	4	11	18	25
D	5	12	19	26
F	6	13	20	27
S	7	14	21	28

40. Woche · Zinstage 277-83
Sonnabend
7
OKTOBER

Las exploraciones demostraron que teníamos una casa muy cerca, pero también...

A = 1750 m.

A = 2000 m.

I have never known nor photographed Che;
nevertheless, I am perhaps the only Cuban photographer to have had his image so often before me.
I remember that in 1967, when I was working as a laboratory
assistant at Korda Studio in Havana, Luis Korda, co-owner with
Alberto, succeeded in obtaining several boxes of photography paper-
Russe 40x50cm that had passed the expiration date. He had the intention
of using it to print a selection of photos of Che, including the photo taken by
Alberto the 5th of March 1960. The goal was to sell them via a commercial network
called "El Cartel. Artículos revolucionarios." *
I remember that I had printed more than 100 40x50 cm copies of them as well as several
hundred copies in the 24x36cm format to use as gifts and compromise.
In the spring of 1968, the studio was nationalised by the revolutionary government and closed soon
after. The archives for the negatives of Che and all the work done on the revolution done by Alberto
were transferred to the Office of Historical Affairs, of which the founder and the director of the Photography
Department was Raúl Corrales. Thus it was in this way that all the negatives remained under his supervision
and care.
After the nationalization of the studio, Alberto worked as an underwater photographer at the Institute of Oceanography,
Luis Korda at the weekly *Palante* and myself as photographer for the review *Cuba Internacional*. We would remain always
very close, personally and professionally speaking, but we would no longer talk about the photos taken of Che. In 1969,
already working as a photographer for the review *Cuba Internacional*, I had the occasion to do a reportage on Che in
the Sierra Maestra, next to journalists Felix Guerra and Froilan Escobar and the sketch artist José Luis Posada. This
assignment would last more than three months and was actually two different trips. We would cover all the important
places where Che stayed, we met all the peasants and combattants who knew him, and from this adventure was born
a Special Edition of the review *Cuba Internacional* entitled *Che Sierra Maestra*.
In 1978, we participated in the First Latin-American Photography Conference in Mexico City. Alberto returned to
his historic negatives to which he had access thanks to Celia Sanchez Manduley, secretary of the State Council in
charge of the file, and with the help of Raúl Corrales, Director of the Photographic Archives of the Historical Affairs
Office. I saw again the negatives that I had manipulated so often in the 60s. At that time, Alberto didn't have a
real dark room, he therefore used mine in my apartment in Vedado. Yet another time, this time as a volunteer,
I often shouldered the responsibility as printer of these famous photos for expositions or just to sell. Several
times people asked me how many times I had printed and reprinted these photos. My answer was always the
same : "I don't have the slightest idea. I can only tell you that I have always had Che in front of me."
In 2002, I decided to regroup the photos realised during the numerous years during which this famous photo
was manipulated and to show them. Result : Che is still in front of me.

José Alberto Figueroa
La Havana, January 2003

• NDT : The poster. Revolutionary Articles.

José Alberto Figueroa
Born the 26th of September 1946 in Havana.
1962-68. Photographer and assistant to Korda.
1969-76. Graphic Reporter. Collaborates for the review
Cuba Internacional.
1981. Member of the Photography Department of the
Union of Cuban Writers and Artists (UNEAC).
1982-83. War correspondant in Angola.

f i g u e r o a

122 ▶

108

L E G

1,2. Che and sensitivity, Alberto Granado, Havana, the 1st of December 2002.
3. Ernesto and le Petiso with the cousins of Alberto Rosario.
4. Letter to Alberto Granado.
5. Ernesto and le Petiso on the raft "Mambo-Tango", 1952, the Amazon.
6. Ernesto and le Petiso in front of the truckers house in Puc.
7. Ernesto and le Petiso with helmets on, with la Norton, January 1952.
8. Temuco, Chili, the 12th of February 1952.
9. Ernesto and le Petiso playing rugby with students from Cordoba.

Korda :
10,11. May 1960, funeral procession for the victims of the assault of the cargo ship "La Coubre".
12,18,19. The 29th of March 1961, the Colinas de Villareal Countryclub in Havana.
13,20,21. May 1960, the "Ernest Hemingway"swordfish fishing tournament, Havana.
14,16. May 1961, visit to Nicaro, Holguin.
15. J.P. Sartre and Simone de Beauvoir at the National Bank.
17. Thursday, the 7th of February 1963, Che harvesting sugar cane with a harvester.

Corrales :
22. Prints from one of the rolls of film taken the 14th of September 1959 in Havana during the first presentation of Che on TV as Director of Industrialisation of the INRA (National Institute of Agricultural Reform).
23,24,25,26,27,29,30,31,32,33. The 14th of September 1959, Havana. First presentation of Che on TV as Director of Industrialisation of the INRA (National Institute of Agricultural Reform).
28,35. May 1959, Revolution Plaza, Havana. Welcome meeting for Fidel upon his return from his travels in the Americas.
34,36. 1960. Havana Airport. Goodbye ceremony for Anastas Mikoyan.

Chinolope :
37. Havana, 2003. Words written by Chinolope in tribute of Che.
38. 1960. Che Guevara at the University of Havana, Cuba.

Liborio Noval :
39,41,45,47. The 26th of February 1961. Marti quarter, construction of houses for those living in the "slums" (Che's first time as a volunteer since his nomination to the post of Minister of Industry).
40,43. May 1961. Volunteer work on the Sierra Maestra embankment in the Port of Havana.
42. September 1963. Che Guevara signing the assistance paper for volunteer work at the edition house Omega.
44.October 1964. Che Guevara inaugurating the "Alfredo Gamonal" factory.
46. December 1961. Che Guevara with Celia Sanchez at Revolution Plaza, Havana. Closing ceremony of the Year of Literacy.
48. August 1961. Che saying goodbye before leaving for Montevideo, Uruguay in order to participate in the Conference of Punta del Este. (Che speaking with Fidel, on his left, and with Captain Antonio Nunez Jimenez.)
49. May 1962. Founding of the section "Partido Unido de la Revolucion Socialista Cubana" (United Party of the Cuban Socialist Revolution).
50. January 1964. Che Guevara with a camera using a telephoto lens. At his side, Bias Roca. In the background, Carlos Rafael Rodriguez. The old woman with the scarf sitting behind Bias Roca is Dolores Ibarruri, known as "La Pasionaria".
51. January 1959. Arrival of Che's parents and brothers from Argentina.
52. September 1962. Arrival of Che Guevara from Moscow.
53. May 1962. Che Guevara giving a conference at the University of Havana.
54. January 1964. Parade in commemoration of the 5th Anniversary of the Revolution. Che Guevara with a movie camera.
55,57. 1961. Che Guevara on the television program *Universidad Popular*.
56. December 1963. Che Guevara in a session of the Worker's Central of Cuba *la Centrale de travailleurs de Cuba*.
58. November 1961, Havana.

Osvaldo Salas :
59,60,61,65. 1961. Marti quarter (First volunteer work of Che's since his nomination as Minister of Industry). Havana.
62. 1960.
63. 1961. Havana.
64. May 1960. Havana.
66. July 1964. Santiago de Cuba.

Salitas, R. Corrales and Liborio, friends for life.

Liborio, R. Corrales, Salitas, Perfecto, Figueroa and Chinolope. "The photographers" next to "El Petiso" Granado.

© Saúl Corral

© Saúl Corral

E   N   D

67. 1964. Revolution Plaza in Havana.
68. The 28th of March 1960. Havana.
69. 1963. Revolution Plaza in Havana.

Roberto Salas :
70. December 1961. Revolution Plaza in Havana.
71. 1962, Che Guevara in a session of the Worker's Central of Cuba.
72. 1963.
73. Revolution Plaza.
74. The 1st of May 1964. Revolution Plaza in Havana.
75. 1963. Havana.

Perfecto Romero :
76. Che during a meeting at La Cabana, January 1959.
77. Che with a box of cigars in his office at La Cabana, 1959.
78. Che on the slopes of the Pic Gavilan in l'Escambray. November 1958.
79. Che and Aleida in the office at La Cabana, 1959.
80. Che at the Camp Leoncio Vidal, Santa Clara, December 1958.
81. Che at the Silueta Barracks, December 1958.
82. Che with his daughter Celia in his house in Neuvo Vedado, 1962.
83. Fidel Castro and Che in the office at La Cabana, January 1959.
84. Funeral procession for the victims of the sabotage of the cargo ship "La Coubre", the 4th of March 1960. Fidel Castro, Ernesto Guevara, Augusto Martinez Sanchez and Antonio Nunez Jimenez.
85. Che with graphic workers at the print shop for the review Carteles, 1960.
86. Che's trip to Argentina. At his side, the Commander Pinero (Barba Roja). 1960.
87. Che cutting sugar cane at the sugar factory "Martinez Prieto", 1962.
88. Camilo Cienfuegos and Che wearing each other's hats (Che wearing Camilo's cowboy hat and Camilo wearing Che's beret).
89. Che playing a game of chess in "la Ciudad Deportiva" (Sports Palace), 1961.
90. Che at the print shop for the review Carteles, 1960.
91. Che giving a conference on television, 1960.
92. Che giving a conference to the Ministry of Industries, 1961.

Roger Pic :
93,94,95,96,97,98,99,100,101,102,103. Photos taken in Cuba by Roger Pic between 1963 and 1964.

La Grafica :
104. Silk-screen print of Che by Arcay.
105. Raúl Martinez's Jornada del Guerrillero Heróico
106. Raúl Martinez's Che with Stars
107. Raúl Martinez's They are the Cuban Revolution
108. Frédéric Brandon's Che for the biography written by Jean Cormier.
109. Another edition of Raúl Martinez's Jornada del Guerrillero Heróico
110. Proposed front cover for this book sketched by Frédéric Brandon, during his trip from Paris to La Rochelle with Jean Cormier and Saul Corrales. The 26th of February 2003.
111. Burri's inscription in a book he gave to Corrales in Paris in 1992.
112. Contact prints from a roll of film taken the 14th of September 1959. Author : Raúl Corrales.
113. Newspaper clippings from the journal Granma, Edition 1, 1st year. Fidel included Che's "goodbye" letter on the day when the Central Committee of the Communist Party of Cuba was present. Letter from Che to Fidel.
114. Photograph taken by R. Corrales during the ceremony where Fidel announced to the Cuban people the death of Che Guevara.

René Burri :
115. January 1963, interview in Look Magazine.
116. Che's journal.
117. La Higuera, where Che was arrested, Bolivia.

José A. Figueroa :
118. New York. September 2001.
119. Anonymous Cuban painter. Havana. 1997.
120. Along the highway between Havana and Matanzas. 1991.
121. Linea Street. Havana. 1996.
122. Vedado. Havana. 1991.
123. Wristwatch with Che's image. 1998.
124. Place de la Cathédrale. Havana. 1989.
125. Reina Street. Havana. 1992.
126. Zippo Lighter, limited edition (only 100 made). Havana. 2000.